SIGNS
&
STREET FURNITURE
IN YORKSHIRE

by
E. ALAN JONES

HUTTON PRESS

2001

Published by

The Hutton Press Ltd.,
130 Canada Drive, Cherry Burton,
Beverley, East Yorkshire
HU17 7SB

Printed and bound by
Fretwells Limited, Hull

ISBN 1 902709 12 8

FOREWORD

By Mr. John Richardson
Formerly senior journalist Yorkshire Evening Press and Gazette and Herald.

Most of us have lazy eyes.

They see for us but we seldom make them look. If they cast around above ground-floor level, as this book does, they will see an intriguing world – albeit a disappearing one – of self-projection and commercial flair.

Today's marketing men may believe they discovered the art. But it has been there for generations. All the better, most would agree, for its simplicity and its direct appeal.

Long before the Town and Country Planning Act, well ahead of the dread word 'precedent', businessmen of vision hired the skills of craftsmen to tell their story.

'Signs and Street Furniture' expands the chapter and verse of that fascinating story, brought to life by an expert in an illustrated study of the way things were.

Long before the paper-boy has called, Alan, as signwriter, is up his ladder chalking the letters of his next commission. Left until later in the morning, his concentration could be suspect. People will chat to him. He is that sort of character.

To a journalist like me Alan Jones is a minor treasure. His workshop is seldom without a story. He opens his door and his heart to anyone prepared to listen.

For those among us with tunnel vision, his book is a delightful eye opener.

John Richardson

To
Jack, Sam, Joe, Charlie, Alfie and Annie-Rose
my grandchildren.

CONTENTS

ACKNOWLEDGEMENTS

Tourist Information Centres at Harrogate and Skipton.

Peter Smith Photography.

The Hutton Press.

Colab Ltd.

Wood Visual Communications for photographs on pages 24, 65, 81, 86/87.

Jim Varney for photograph on page 13.

John Richardson formerly of the York & County Press.

Assistants Pat Jones, Patrick Revis, Gill Milner.

Kirklees Metropolitan Council.

The Knaresborough Story (Mr. Arnold Kellett).

The York & County Press for some photographs.

Michael Scales Photography (page 71 photograph).

Yorkshire Regional Newspapers Ltd. (Back Cover photograph).

INTRODUCTION

The high street as we know it with its many shops, restaurants and public houses has taken shape over many years.

The Romans, Normans and Anglo Saxons gradually developed a pattern for villages and towns throughout the land. Initially, a stall would be set up outside a house of anyone wishing to sell goods or items made on the premises. Then as trade improved, and to save bringing the stall indoors each evening, an opening onto the street from the downstairs room would be opened during the day. The purchaser would stand on the street and transact the business without ever going inside the premises.

Salesmen would still travel round the countryside selling goods from a wholesaler. The public would never get the chance to buy direct from the producer.

Market towns developed around cattle buying and selling Country folk would bring produce like butter, eggs and cheese to offer for sale also.

Gradually, in the towns of the 18th century, shops were designed to allow customers actually to go inside to view the goods prior to purchase. To identify these premises to a people that could hardly read, signs with drawings of easily recognised symbols were erected above the premises. As well as the sign, a small display would be placed in the window at street level.

As the commercial methods of manufacture and distribution of goods developed in the late 18th and early 19th century, more and more shops opened selling a larger variety of items.

Services like pawnbrokers, barbers, bakers were all competing with the haberdasher and ironmonger for the public's patronage. This competition required larger signs and advertisements in the local newspapers and on handbills posted around the area.

Today it is interesting to look above the first floor fascia level and see how the premises may have looked a hundred years ago. Modern shop fronts, in the main, are not of architectural interest and are designed only to show off the displays to the greatest advantage. Many high streets now look alike with the national chains of shops branching out all over the country.

The signwriter, who worked only by hand, has now to supply cut out or moulded plastic letters and needs to understand the workings of a computer to assist with the design, supply and layout of modern lettering. It is good to notice that the demand for quality gold leaf work on fascia or window is still in demand, so it will be many years before the signwriter's services are not required. I do hope so . . . as I am a signwriter!!

The contents of this book are intended to show a few items of interest in the Yorkshire area and to encourage the reader to go out and see the different designs and buildings for him or herself. Looking and comparing old photographs with what is there today sometimes shows very little change above first floor level. It is the view from street level that has changed most. Since the advent of 'Town Planners' it remains a mystery to me how some of the properties have been allowed to develop in their present state to be a blot on the street scene.

E. Alan Jones
Signs Malton
June 2001

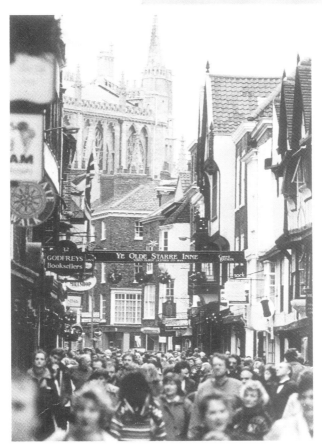

THE STREET SCENE

The pedestrian street contains many very old buildings and examples of carving and gilding at first floor levels. Ye Olde Starre Inne in York sign is a rare example of a sign that stretches fully across a street. Made of wood and hand lettered with a gold leaf 'Star' above the capital 'S'.

Goodramgate, York photographed in 1893.
The total lack of traffic, and customers, is interesting in this photograph.
The prices could not be painted direct onto the shop fronts today with the constant increases.

Yorkersgate, Malton c.1904.
This scene has altered little architecturally over the years. Note the interest of everyone in the setting up of the plate camera and tripod.
   Mr. John Richardson's office (the writer of my foreword) was just past the Hairdressing Room's sign to the right of the picture.

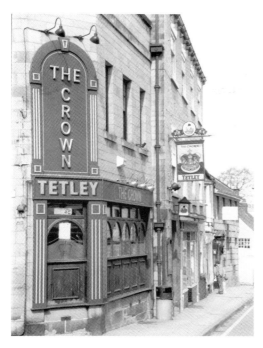

The use of a corner site to display raised half round lettering. These letters were made from solid mahogany and finished in gold leaf but nowadays are usually formed in plastic.

The fascia and illuminated lamp sign also help to identify these premises.

Market Place, Hull c.1900.
Horse-drawn and hand barrows fully evident on a busy market day. All manner of goods would be traded from the country hinterland and also from the then busy port.

Ramsden House Murals.
The mural on the end of the Ramsden House, Huddersfield which overlooks Ramsden Street traces pictorially the development of the woollen industry from a cottage craft, practised as an ancillary to farming, up to the beginning of the industrial revolution. The artist is a local man, Mr. Harold Blackburn. The mural measures 65 feet long and 8 feet high.

Life in the back streets of our cities at the turn of the century must have been very grim.

There would be no running water or inside toilets to the houses and the only space for children to play would be in the narrow cobbled street area. A single gas light illuminates the scene.

Setts, or cobbles, are shown again in this early photograph of Beverley Market Place. Everything here is very much the same today and a busy stall market takes place every Saturday.

Setts are in evidence again in Malton Market Place. The old Town Hall in the centre of the photograph shows the filled-in archways that used to be an open butter market.

The Bull Inn is the white building to the right of the Town Hall later demolished to make way for Newgate.

The Balloon Yeast Company, named on the carrier's vehicle is now the business premises of Paul Beanland & Associates, Estate Agents on the other side of the Market Place near the Church.

Large market squares were needed as all the activities like cattle and horse sales took place in this area. Many of the towns in Yorkshire, and supposedly elsewhere, have this large open space in their town centres. Thirsk, shown here, is a good example.

The narrow streets of Sedbergh are still cobbled with overhanging shops, wrought iron railings and unfortunately, modern traffic.

A narrow area of Hornsea shows traffic lights, seat, litter bin, electric control box for lights. Shop fascia signs and a wall lettered sign add character to the area.

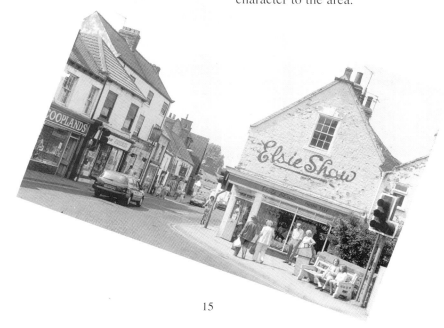

Northallerton, a modern market town shows how people and traffic have changed what would have been a large open square.

Tall street lamps, car park spaces, telephone kiosk, litter bins and very wide pedestrian walkways with centre lamps.

Modern shop fascias are mainly glass and plastic with a large unnecessary canopy spoiling an otherwise long line of shop fronts.

A town bank would in the past house the bank manager and his family. Ornate door and window arches at all levels with the modern night safe and money machine discretely fitted into the wall at ground level. This example is from Thirsk.

Whilst the sign letters will be illuminated from within each letter they have been tastefully designed to suit the building and its surroundings.

TRADE DISPLAYS

Free standing hand carved figure with open snuff box outside a tobacconists in York.

Made from wood and sealed with oil based primer, undercoat and gloss in bright colours to attract custom.

Proprietor and staff proudly pose outside this draper's emporium in the West Riding with what looks like a special display for the photographer.

Pattern books, bale of cloth near door and garments and caps hung outside.

All items used and needed by the farming community are displayed outside the premises of this agricultural merchant. R. Yates & Sons, Malton.

Butter churns, pig troughs, sack barrows, turnip choppers, wire netting, ploughs and many other household items.

Inman Brothers certainly put on a display for this photograph taken about 1920. All tickets show that the animal in question was a prize winner in the local fatstock market.

Notice the dry cured hams and bacon sides between the upstairs windows.

The ceramic pastoral scenes at the base of the windows at ground level are virtually unseen in today's modern shop front designs.

Small lean-to shop adjacent to owner's dwelling provides a nice setting for a pet store.

The eye is attracted to the fruit displayed in front of this small shop window. Without this display one could easily miss the premises in Masham altogether.

Old fashioned bookshop in what was a butcher's shop in The Shambles, Malton.

Decorative display that adds a little interest and colour to the street scene.
This is claimed to be the smallest Bookshop in the country.

Buckets, spades, rubber rings and specialist gift items for the seaside holiday-maker in Whitby.

All bright and eyecatching set in a kiosk at the harbour side.

K. & K. Hunt's premises, in Askrigg, is typical of a village shop except that the right hand window had a permanent display of old fashioned items when the television series 'All Creatures Great and Small' was being filmed in the area as it was very often seen in a background shot.

Two very different shop fronts. The top one in Malton is modern with a complete fibreglass moulding painted spruce green and hand lettered with gold leaf.

The bottom shop in Northallerton is beautifully incised lettering filled with gold leaf from a bygone era.

SIGN LETTERING

Bishops' mitre shaped signboards, superbly signwritten on a maroon base and very suitable for the profession advertised.

Wall lettered signs are not as popular as they used to be. The technique was to establish the size of the area to be lettered and square it down to a manageable size on paper. Then draw out the wording on a smaller paper plan so that it looked right. Take this pattern up the scaffolding to the job and scale up again *insitu*. An early example from York.

Window lettering is an art in itself. Usually completed by the signwriter from the inside of the window.

This means making a paper pattern to the exact size of the text and fixing it to the outside of the glass.

Clean the inside of the glass and then paint the letters following the pattern that can be seen through the glass. Sealed with oil paint and varnished, this lettering should last for years.

Just out of interest, notice the vertical lettering to the right of the picture. Whilst very well executed, and filling the only space available, it does show how difficult this lettering can be to read. This example is from Northallerton.

Classics Menswear, Richmond, with logo is in machine cut vinyl and fixed either on the inside or the outside of the glass. This method of lettering also needs a very clean window and will stand the usual washing and cleaning. Much of the temporary signwork we see on films and television is done in this way and can be easily removed if required.

Freestanding signboards are not popular generally with local councils because they are deemed to be a pedestrian hazard.

Whilst this may or may not be so, they do serve as a very noticeable advert placed at right angles to the business premises.

Traditionally made of timber and painted by hand with the trader's message, the modern varieties can be fibre glass or metal hand lettered or silk screen printed.

The public could not mistake the symbol outside the tea shop in Muker. A superb old kettle swings invitingly from a wrought iron support, welcoming visitors.

The freestanding sign in Dent is shaped like a cottage loaf thus telling the prospective customer what to find inside.

Cellar Antiques of Hawes leaves one in no doubt as to their trade, with a freestanding sign leaning against the barrel and the wall sign along with antiques on display. The open low door with the steps leading into the unknown, makes even the least curious person interested to view.

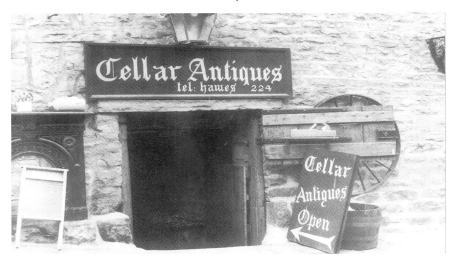

Figureheads, reminiscent of the old sailing ship days, stand guard at each side of this fish and chip shop in Whitby.

Highly ornate, and when original, carved from timber, painted and gilded. Nowadays however, many such items are produced by making a mould from an original and casting in fibre glass as many similar ones as are required. Whilst painted with oil-based paints in the same way as the wooden ones, they seem to lack the character of the original one-off.

Well produced, easy to read, signs leaving no doubt as to the trade or calling of the business premises in Hawes (above) and Thirsk (right).

Doctors' surgeries need to inform patients of their opening times and where someone can be contacted in an emergency.

Sometimes a joiner would make timber signs painted and lettered because the times may alter. If confident that things will remain the same for the foreseeable future then an engraved sign may be used.

Whilst the law states that a premises selling alcohol must display the name of the licensee holder, it is most unusual to see methylated spirits mentioned in this context.

Both these examples are from Masham.

A large cut out dachshund forms the basis for this interesting signboard for a pet food shop in Richmond. Shaped signs are usually cut from exterior quality plywood of a suitable thickness. Birch faced plywood being by far the best with a nice smooth grain for painting. Seal all edges and paint all over with oil based primer, undercoat and gloss prior to lettering.

These premises in Kirkbymoorside still display the old trade sign of a Silk Mercer whilst not actually practicing it. How nice to see this retained.

Many shop entrances used for advertising decorative mosaics. This method uses small coloured glazed pottery tiles to be set in shapes, letters and patterns with a level top surface.

The tiles were glazed so that the area could be walked on and also kept clean. This example is from Thirsk.

Leaded windows were, as the name suggests, pieces of either plain or coloured glass set into strips of lead to fill the window area. Sometimes known as leaded lights. This is an art now becoming popular again but with very few trades-people able to continue this ancient craft.

Prior to this being laid outside a shop in Leyburn, Messrs Wilson Dentist must have had a very professional looking frontage.

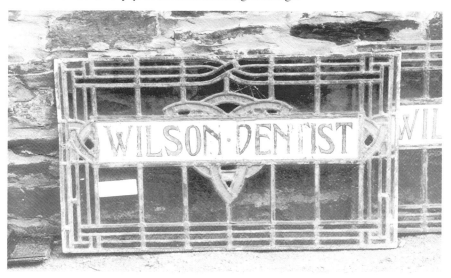

Mr. F. Moore of Howden shows the old-fashioned display window that opened directly onto the street.

Also, what better to display your name and trade than to set it in large glazed tiles into the frontage.

This large carved crest set into the wall of premises in Fossgate, York would have been carved at ground level and then fixed above the doorway. Very decorative wall bracket lamp and also smaller sign bracket.

Notice also the small alarm bell box that is sadly a sign of our times.

HOTEL & INN SIGNS

Prior to the wide footpath one would assume that this canopy offered shelter to the alighting passengers in the horse-drawn carriage age.

Topped off with a wrought iron surround rail and flower boxes is the very majestic Golden Lion of Northallerton.

Tucked in between two more modern buildings, this grand Tudor style inn in Northallerton offers the traveller good food and traditional ale.

It is to be hoped that pigeon pie is not on the menu if you look at the small ledge at the top of the photograph!

Black Bulls are very popular for inn names and signs.

Reeth's Black Bull is hundreds of years old and well worth a visit to sample the very old world charm of large log fires and stone-flagged floors.

The ground floor bow windows are from the days when this part of the property was a draper's shop and has since been added into the pub area now as a lounge.

A cut-out metal silhouette bull is suspended by an ornate wrought iron support as the main sign.

The Theakston's Brewery at Masham chose the Black Bull for their 'in house' pub name.

Looking out over Thirsk's market square, this friendly hand-painted fellow offers a welcome.

A cut out board, with the Black Bull painted on it, is fixed to a background board which in turn is fixed to the wall.

Hand-painted pictorial direct onto the rendered wall surface.

Letters fixed in raised locators to give a three-dimensional shadow to the Coach & Horses at Tadcaster.

The same effect as above but with extended locators on each letter to give a very pleasing result when the sun casts its shadow on the white wall surface of this Muker public house.

Famous Knaresborough Inn named after John Metcalf, better known as 'Blind Jack'. Losing his sight at 6 years old in 1723, due to smallpox, he never let this stop him leading a normal life. As a child, he would guide people round the town every night.

A brilliant musician on the fiddle and oboe for the Knaresborough Volunteers. A horse dealer, carrier, fishmonger and stagecoach operator, but mainly known for his road building along with Mr. Macadam.

Carved winged angel heralding the customers to the Angel & White Horse Inn, Tadcaster.

Hand painted signboard suspended from a wrought iron bracket with floodlighting from the base upwards.

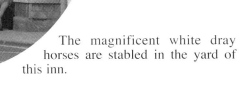

The magnificent white dray horses are stabled in the yard of this inn.

Ornate double-sided sign on the front of a Tudor style building complete with timber jibbet. Illuminated lamp sign and overhead spots complete the advertising for the Rose & Crown in Hornsea.

Clear, easy to read, pub sign with pictorial and brewery name.

First class pictorial work by John Creighton, the local signwriter in Kirkbymoorside, North Yorkshire. His artistic talent was inherited from his late father, Lewis Creighton.

Lewis is seen posed in the doorway, not leaving or entering! He was well known internationally as 'The Moorland Artist' due to his capturing the spirit of the North York Moors in his oil paintings. Latterly, he had also been painting in watercolour to an even higher standard.

Wrought iron and plate glass canopy with hand-lettered title in Huddersfield.

The hand-dressed quoin stones make for a very impressive hotel frontage.

Unusual feature outside the very old Black Swan Inn is this beam and shelf arrangement. Maybe at one time this was actually inside and not open to the elements.

Artwork is believed to be by the late Mr. George Bower from Pickering who, in my opinion, was the best exponent of the signwriter's art this area has ever seen.

STREET FURNITURE

Betty's famous café in Harrogate, with wrought iron Victorian canopy and the gold leaf logo and lettering on the shop windows.

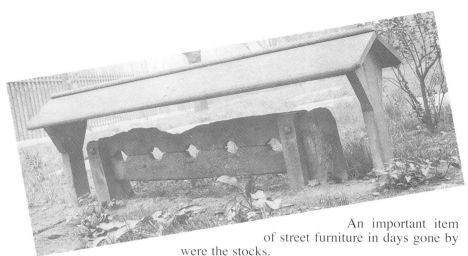

An important item
of street furniture in days gone by
were the stocks.

One, two or three persons could be placed by the neck, arms, or legs, into these wooden clamps.

The wrong-doer would be left in these stocks for a given time and pelted with rotten vegetables, or worse, to humiliate him for his misdemeanour.

A lot could be said in favour of this deterrent today.

The stocks that were in The Holy Trinity Churchyard in York would not have had the protective cover when actually in use. This was added later to protect the museum piece from the weather.

Stocks, steps, wrought iron railings all outside The Black Bull Inn, Haworth, West Yorkshire.

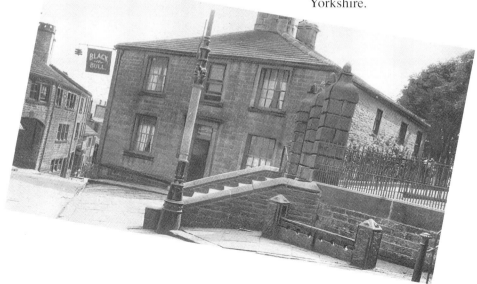

Everyday items on the quayside at any fishing port would be crab and lobster pots along with wood or cast iron bollards to tie the fishing boats to.

A more recent item of seaside furniture is the pay-as-you-view telescope. Two steps are provided for adults and children to stand on to view the boats or people on the pier or sands.

Wrought iron gates and ornamentation show the craftsman's skill. Much of this has to be modern as the majority was removed by government order during the Second World War to provide armaments.

Modern ironwork scrolls in the main are spot-welded where they touch each other. In older work, it was either joined by fire welding or clips. A fine example from Kendall's Yard in Skipton.

This very old ironwork would survive the cutting torch during the Second World War because it was protecting cellar steps. The gate at the top has to be locked and just above the gate is an unusual iron wall support.

The barley sugar style posts are of interest here and would be cast in a sand mould. The metal being poured in when molten and then the sand being broken away after cooling to reveal the finished object.

The raised wall capping is unusual to support the railings.

An elegant street scene in Harrogate, with front and step railings.

Ironwork comes in many forms, as this modern sculpture on Hull Docks shows.

An older use of iron was to act as a brace for bridge coping stones as seen here in Malham Village. The blacksmith would provide the ironwork and the stonemason carve out holes in the stone. Usually, the holes were filled with molten lead after the iron had been inserted. When the lead had cooled everything was a good tight fit.

Old lamp standard in Harrogate, with cast wine leaves as a pattern in contrast to the modern bicycle stands.

Craftsmen-made house gates incorporating all manner of animals and birds found in the vicinity.

Lamps and lampposts have a long history. First lit by tallow and oil, then gas and now electricity.

Converted lamp from gas to electricity at Howden, East Yorkshire.

Unusual but most decorative cast lamp at Red Beck Cottages, Horsforth, West Yorkshire.

A canal side lamp holder at Skipton. This could be one of the oil filled lamps that were placed on site when dark and removed the following day for refilling and wick trimming.

Bridge lamp over the River Foss in York, showing the four gas mantles inside.

Neat example of a modern litter bin placed unobtrusively at Whitby.

The modern finger post is designed for however many directions are needed. Easily altered both for lettering and direction. A good example from Knaresborough.

Modern cast street furniture, either in metal or fibre glass, looks very much in keeping with old or new surroundings. The litter bins usually have a lift out container inside that the local authority can empty and replace.

An engineering feat in Whitby showing the 199 steps and adjacent footsteps and roadway. Observe how worn each end of the large steps are near the handrail, showing that many thousands of feet have passed this way to the Abbey and Church at the top.

The donkey has the advantage of raised cobbles on his roadway but, even so, it is very steep.

Iron spikes prevent people standing or sitting on the bank premises.

Apart from a very well-stocked Provision Merchant's window in Hawes, the guard rail is unique and serves as a protection for the large plate glass area.

Originally, milestones were actually stone but as time progressed wood and metal ones were also used.

As this marker near Sedbergh, on the Dent road, shows all that is needed is the 'S' for Sedbergh and the '4' for miles.

This direction post in Harrogate is far more explicit and gives mileage and road location.

To know that they were 220 miles from London must have been a great comfort to travellers looking at this cast iron marker in Thirsk, North Yorkshire. They would have to guess how far they were from Easingwold!

During early days in towns and villages there would be no drinking water in the houses. Communal pumps and even the collection of rainwater would be the only source.

Village pump at Hutton Rudby. This was a fairly traditional style with the lead cast workings encased in a timber cladding. The handle has been fixed down for safety.

This standpipe in Reeth, erected in 1868, explains on its plaque; This water was brought into the town and these tanks erected by the munification of

George Robinson ESQ re.

of Richmond

The solid brass plate has been hand engraved in a beautiful script style without any pantograph or machine aid.

Provision of drinking fountains took many forms and some even provided cups.

The Adam Sedgwick memorial stone has a small recess that houses the water fountain. Adam Sedgwick was a geologist and his father the Rev. Richard Sedgwick had been the curate of Dent Parish Church and also a geologist.

The stone at West Witton provides a public water supply but warns on the small tag that the water must be boiled prior to drinking.

Almost twin pillar boxes, but one GvIR and the other EIIR, at Knaresborough.

Twin letter boxes at Skipton Post Office. More and more offices now have two boxes so the public can sort their mail into 1st and 2nd class at the time of posting.

Many buildings have sundials on them. As well as being decorative if set correctly, one can also tell the time from the shadow cast by the light over the raised armature. A good example from Richmond.

Clocks and signs are not usually hung together on the same support frame, but this is a very good example of a neat, and easy to read sign, and a good clear-faced timepiece over a Northallerton premises.

In the horse-drawn days, mounting blocks or stones were positioned along the routes to enable riders to mount. Many survive as illustrated in Dent, but may be disguised with tubs and flowers and not readily identifiable.

Seats are provided by municipal and district authorities for the public's benefit in wood, iron or concrete.

These two examples, in Harrogate, have cast iron supports and wooden seats. The top photograph shows clearly the maker's name the lower photograph uses the serpent form to ward off evil spirits.

Shelters may still be found mainly in seaside spa towns. These two-sided shelters with a middle divider protected the occupants whichever way the wind may be blowing. Sometimes plain and sometimes ornate but very Victorian in their origin, Whitby above, Harrogate below.

Cluster of bricks forming what looks like four individual chimney stacks.

Slate and brick chimney of unusual design.

The builder of this property made his permanent mark in 1890 by raising the bricks to make an image in this end wall.

Helmsley to Lord Feversham.

Memorials are very much part of the street scene and may be erected to one well-known individual or to people from the area lost in action during a war.

Erected in 1865 to Sir Tatton Sykes, shows men of the East Yorkshire Regiment at arms and with their everyday work tools.

The Queen Victoria Memorial in Bradford.

Market day in old Richmond with a modern photograph taken from the top of the castle and an older photograph from ground level.

Otley market square at the turn of this century. The wall advert shows that Moss's Tea was "FIRST CROP", this must be the best quality.

Two quiet village locations for War Memorials, Gillamoor and West Bretton.

Most market crosses appear to have four steps up to them but there is no known reason for this. Howden to the left, Masham to the right.

Always found in the town's market square and usually the centre of all activity. Kirkbymoorside below.

Dents, Commercial Street, Norton, Malton. Taken by Harry Edwards early last century showing goods displayed on footpath, sack wheels and everyday street scene.

Sun Hotel. Interesting signs in Wheelgate, Malton early 1900's.

FILM LOCATIONS

Filming 'All Creatures Great and Small' in Malton, May 1974. The star of the film Simon Ward is looking in shop window.

Film companies use many locations and properties when on outside locations. Two of the 'Skeldale" houses from the film and television series 'All Creatures Great and Small' are shown here.

Reeth house used in the film.

Askrigg house used in the television series.

Old photograph of Askrigg centre with the same house as above, to the right of shot.

Holmfirth is a tourist centre due to the television series 'Last of the Summer Wine'.

Freestanding board shows the trio with a cut out Compo proudly standing to the rear.

Nora Batty and Compo's house up the steps. The additional signs are for businesses that operate when filming is not taking place, making the most of the location's fame.

Sid's Café was a paint store in Holmfirth but is now a real life café when not needed as a set for the filming of the popular television series.

Nick Berry in 'Heartbeat' whilst filming in Goathland.

Temporary signs on the village shop in Goathland for the 'Heartbeat' series.

SIGNS &
UNUSUAL ITEMS

The hand cart was often in evidence in any city street early last century. Here is a fine example of the signwriter's skill in using the available space.

Neat, easily read layout with municipal crest and scrolls. The letters neatly shaded to give a three-dimensional effect.

Note the paper labels and wired tops of the milk bottles of that period.

Now you see me . . . now you don't!

The dark area at the corner of the two buildings is, in fact, a passageway in Easingwold.

Entering the passage from other side.

Exiting passage from the top photo side.

Seats are traditionally placed under trees and this tree, in Hutton Rudby, looks to have objected!

Denby Dale great pie dish of 1964 now filled with flowers outside the village inn in the main street.

The feast, held periodically for over 200 years, and a pie of this size prepared and baked for charitable purposes.

Derek Fox, friendly Malton butcher, uses his shop bike as a way to advertise his business.

Sportsgrounds, clubs and towns all have
their signs to advertise who they are and when their
next events are being held.

Wonderful trade advertising on the firm's fleet of delivery vehicles in the West Riding.

Good clear lettering, and one could suppose, full of colour.

The double-sided advert board on the roof is set diagonally to give a clearer message in transit and also to offer less wind resistance.

This fractured lettering presents a problem for the signwriter who has to work this by hand. The designer on the computer can sometimes make life difficult!

Modern cast acrylic letters complement the old-fashioned objects in this garden shop.

Whilst not really signs or street furniture, these two photographs show how two buildings appear to have been built in what was a gap between two other properties.

The top photograph uses the idea of a tall thin building as the trading name for their fashion business in Knaresborough. The bottom photograph is of a building in Masham.

Raised and decorative brickwork adds interest to this corner site.

The filled-in window now provides a suitable area to display the gun, fish and lettering. Dogs' heads in three-dimension on the hanging sideboard prove to be an imaginative use of the space available.

The law does not allow bookmakers and amusement caterers to have open display windows onto the street. The idea being that underage youngsters cannot be tempted inside.

This very classy display masks the amusement arcade.

This most modern phone box is open-sided and made from very strong materials to try and make it vandal proof.

The novelty with this new-style street toilet is that you select your requirement from the panel at the side and insert your money into the slot. The door opens and in you go into a centrally heated chamber. The cabin contains a washbasin with hot water and soap and when the customer comes out the whole lot flushes and washes inside.